NEW TECHNOLOGY

energy technology

Chris Oxlade

Evans

Published by Evans Brothers Limited

© 2008 Evans Brothers Ltd

Evans Brothers Limited
2A Portman Mansions
Chiltern Street
London W1U 6NR

First published 2008

British Library Cataloguing in Publication Data
Oxlade, Chris
    Energy technology. - (New technology)
    1. Energy industries - Technological innovations - Juvenile literature 2. Energy development - Juvenile literature
    I. Title
    621'.042

    ISBN 9 780 23753 430 1

Printed in China

Credits
Series Editor: Paul Humphrey
Editor: Gianna Williams
Designer: Keith Williams
Production: Jenny Mulvanny
Picture researchers: Rachel Tisdale
    and Laura Embriaco

Acknowledgements
Title page and p.24 Verdant Power, Inc.; p.6 Photodisc; p.7 Edward Parker/EASI-Images/CFW Images; p.8 Jan Rysavy/istockphoto.com; p.9 Universal Display; p.10 Oak Ridge National Laboratory; p.11 Ice Energy; p.12 BP; p.13 Vattenfall; p.15 Saras; p.16 Keith Weller/USDA; p.17 Svensk Biogas; p.18 Coppice Resources; p.19 BP; p.21 Ripe Studios/Verdant Power, Inc.; p.22 Ocean Power Delivery; p.23 Ocean Power Technologies, Inc.; p.24 Verdant Power, Inc.; p.25 RE Power; p.26 Chris Rogers/istockphoto.com; p.27 Jurie Maree/istockphoto.com; p.28 Georgia Tech Research Institute; p.29 top Splashpower; p.29 bottom Carla Thomas/NASA/Dryden Flight Research Center; p.31 Toshiba; p.32 Rob Bowden/EASI-Images/CFW Images; p.33 NASA; p.34 Solar Century; p.35 Gary Meek/Georgia Tech Research Institute; p.37 Objetivo; p.38 Martin Rose/Getty Images; p.39 AREVA/Bourdon Paivi; p.40 EFDA-JET; p.41 ITER; p.43 Solar Century.

This book was prepared for Evans Brothers Ltd by Discovery Books Ltd.

contents

introduction

Our modern world could not function without energy. We need energy for our homes, for industries, for transport and for communications. We already need a vast range of methods to produce all this energy. However, if we don't use technology to help us limit the amount of energy we use, we will need to find new ways of producing greater amounts of energy and we will need to produce energy using technology that will not harm the planet.

Energy problems We face two major problems in the next few decades: dwindling supplies of crude oil and global warming. Today, fuels made from oil (such as petrol, diesel, butane and fuel oil) provide more than half our energy. However, many experts think we will begin to face oil shortages within fifty years. So we need to develop new ways of producing energy to replace it.

Millions of lights shine out from the city of Honolulu, Hawaii. Many city office buildings leave lights on overnight, which on a worldwide scale is an enormous waste of precious energy.

HOW IT WORKS

Energy is measured in units called joules (J). The amount of energy all the world's humans use every second is 13 terajoules (13,000,000,000,000 joules). That's enough to keep a light bulb running for 4,000 years. Eighty per cent of this energy comes from fossil fuels. It's estimated that we will need nearly twice as much energy by 2030 unless we develop machines that use less energy and find ways of using energy more wisely.

Global warming is a more threatening problem. Most climatologists agree that the carbon dioxide we release into the atmosphere by burning fossil fuels (known as carbon emissions) is causing global warming. In turn, this is causing climate change. Potential effects of climate change are more frequent storms, flooding, droughts, water shortages and habitat destruction. These are serious problems that could eventually affect the lives of everybody on Earth. We must reduce our carbon emissions by developing technologies that allow fossil fuels to be burned without releasing carbon dioxide, and technologies that can provide renewable energy and help us reduce consumption.

CUTTING EMISSIONS

In 2007, the experts of the Intergovernmental Panel on Climate Change (IPCC) published a report on the potential effects of global warming, and how we must cut carbon emissions in order to halt it. The report says that our carbon emissions must start going down dramatically by 2020. This means we must develop 'low-carbon' technologies straight away.

Climate change is likely to create more extremes of weather, such as the drought that caused this reservoir in Mexico to dry up.

CHAPTER 1
energy efficiency

The simplest way of tackling the problems of pollution and carbon emissions is to save energy by reducing the amount we use. This can be achieved not only by switching off appliances and devices when they are not in use, but also by developing technology to make machines and buildings as energy efficient as possible. Since we have to pay for the energy we use, saving it also has the advantage of saving us money.

Energy-efficient appliances

Appliances from washing machines to computers are increasingly energy efficient, but new technologies are needed to save more energy. For example, a cutting-edge technology that could save 50 per cent of the energy used to run refrigerators and freezers is the vacuum-insulated panel (VIP). This is a thin panel containing a vacuum between two metal plates. It insulates in the same way as a vacuum flask. The vacuum stops heat from outside getting into the appliance.

Changing light bulbs
The incandescent light bulb (the type with a glowing element inside) is one of the greatest energy wasters we have. It converts just five per cent of the electricity supplied to it into light. The rest is turned to heat, which is lost to the air. There are about four billion light bulbs in the USA, and a similar number in Europe. They use about one-fifth of all the electricity we generate. Modern energy-efficient bulbs, called compact fluorescent lamps, are far better, but the best are only 30 per cent efficient. Some countries, including the UK, have decided to allow only energy-efficient bulbs after 2012.

Light-emitting diode (LED) technology is used in modern torches and small lamps, and researchers are

The glowing filament inside an incandescent light bulb converts 95 per cent of electricity into wasted heat.

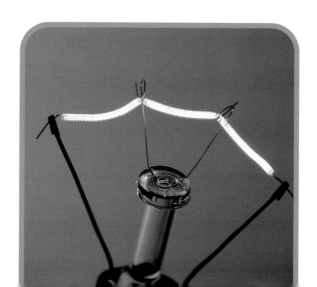

HOW IT WORKS

Light-emitting diodes are microchips made of semiconductor material such as gallium that emits light when electricity flows through it. They produce a large amount of light for their small size. The chip inside a typical LED bulb is just 1 mm across.

now attempting to develop cheap, standard light bulbs based on LEDs. These LED bulbs should last 50 times as long as incandescent bulbs, and could eventually be 70 per cent efficient. They should have replaced other light bulb technologies in five to 20 years' time.

Saving energy at the source

Most electricity is currently produced by burning fossil fuels in electricity generating stations (power stations). In conventional power stations, more than half the energy in the fuels is lost to the atmosphere in the form of heat. The most modern power stations use technology called combined heat and power (CHP), where this waste heat is captured and used for heating houses and businesses. Advanced CHP stations could be up to 70 per cent efficient.

Electricity from power stations is distributed along power lines. Energy is lost here, too, as heat into the air. One future solution to this problem would

WHAT'S NEXT?

An organic light-emitting diode (OLED) is a light-emitting diode that produces light from a layer made up of natural molecules, like those in plastics. An OLED is extremely thin (a hundred could fit across a human hair), and can be made in thin, flexible sheets. General Electric is one company that has developed an OLED lighting panel, but further development is needed to make the panel more reliable and brighter. We may be using OLED lighting within five years.

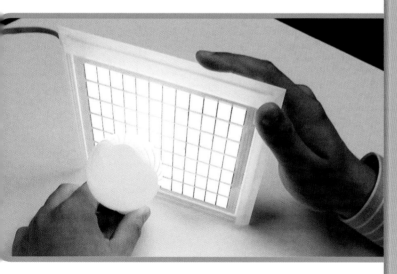

An OLED lighting panel beside a standard light bulb. Panels like this could cover entire walls.

be to use superconducting cables, which have no resistance to electricity and so do not get hot. Another is known as distributed generation. This is where electricity is generated on a small scale in many locations, rather than on a large scale in a few power stations. Distributed generation is beginning to happen. For example, the US Postal Service has installed solar cells at its base in California to produce some of its own energy.

Zero-carbon buildings In buildings, vast amounts of energy are used for heating, air conditioning and lighting. Most of this energy can be saved by using technologies known as passive heating and cooling, and by capturing

HOW IT WORKS

In passive solar heating, sunlight is allowed to enter a building through windows, where it hits walls and floors, both heating the buildings and storing heat. When the Sun goes down, the stored heat is released again to keep the building warm. In passive cooling, window shades keep heat out in the heat of the day, and allow warm air to rise out of the building. Electrochromic glass, or 'smart' glass, darkens when a small electric current is passed through it. It can allow light and heat in, or be switched on to keep heat out.

natural light. The aim for building designers is to eliminate the need for heating and cooling systems that use electricity or fuels. These buildings are known as zero-emission or zero-carbon buildings. Experimental zero-emission homes have been built at the Building Research Establishment in the UK, and by Oak Ridge National Laboratory in the USA.

An experimental zero-carbon house at the Oak Ridge National Laboratory, Tennessee, USA.

Heat in the ground Heating and cooling of a building can also be done with a new technology called a ground-source heat pump. When it's warm, excess heat from the building is stored in the earth and rock in the ground. The heat is passed to the ground through pipes. When it's cold, heat from the ground is pumped back into the building. Ground-source heat pumps are already available to buy, and their use is quickly growing. Pendle Vale College, a 'green' school in Lancashire, England opened in 2008, using GSHP for heating.

WHAT'S NEXT?

Energy is wasted by heating, cooling and lighting parts of buildings that are not in use. Advanced sensing systems track people moving through buildings, and automatically turn heating, cooling and lighting on and off to save energy. These are already installed in hundreds of buildings worldwide. For example, each room of the CrestHill Hotel chain in the USA contains an occupancy sensor. When guests leave the room, the heating and air conditioning are turned down to save energy. Over the coming years, more accurate sensors and more intelligent software will allow these systems to save more and more energy.

Installing the underground coils of pipe for a ground-source heat pump. Water passing through the pipes transfers heat from the ground to the house.

CHAPTER 2
fossil fuels

Coal, oil and gas provide 88 per cent of all our energy, including two-thirds of the electricity we use. Our use of them is predicted to increase over the next few decades. New technologies will allow us to use them more cleanly and efficiently.

Clean-burning coal Coal is the main fuel burned in electricity-generating stations. Poor-quality coal can now be burned more cleanly and efficiently than in the past. This is known as clean-coal technology and it is being developed mainly in Europe, North America and Japan. It reduces pollution by removing gases such as sulphur dioxide and nitrogen monoxide from power station chimneys. As clean-coal technology is developed, it will become more efficient at producing power. It will also reduce carbon emissions.

FINDING FOSSIL FUELS

As reserves of coal, oil and gas are used up, it becomes increasingly hard to find the deposits that are left in the Earth's rocks. New technology is helping to locate and extract these deposits. This includes complex computer models of rock strata (layers), and superships used for drilling in the seabed under the oceans.

Conventional rigs stand on the seabed and cannot work in very deep water. Instead superships work as mobile drilling rigs. They then stay in position automatically during drilling operations.

The Jack Ryan, *a drilling supership, works off the coast of Africa. The central tower supports pipes that drill down into the seabed.*

FOR AND AGAINST

For
- Fossil fuels provide cheap and easy energy in large amounts.
- We can convert the energy in fossil fuels easily into electricity.
- There is plenty of coal left to use.

Against
- Burning fossil fuels releases carbon dioxide, the major cause of global warming.
- Burning fossil fuels produces pollution that causes smog and acid rain.
- Recovering fossil fuels from the ground is difficult and often dangerous.
- Mining destroys huge areas of land.
- Fossil fuels will be more expensive as it gets harder to reach the last remaining deposits.

The supercritical power station at Schwarze Pumpe, Germany, burns low-grade lignite coal cleanly and efficiently.

Super and ultra efficient Old coal fired power stations are only 30 per cent efficient. Now new power stations are being built that use clean-coal technologies. Known as supercritical power stations, they use extra-high-pressure, extra-high-temperature steam to drive their turbines (which in turn drive the electricity generators). Supercritical stations have efficiencies up to 45 per cent. More than 250 are in operation around the world, with the largest being at Schwarze Pumpe in Germany. They are beginning to replace older plants in developing countries. There are now even more efficient power stations called ultrasupercritical stations. They are up to 50 per cent efficient. There are more than 20 in operation in northern Europe, the USA and Japan.

Another clean-coal technology under development is fluidised bed combustion, where the coal burns in a stream of air that keeps it airborne. This makes it burn more efficiently than in a conventional power station, where the coal settles to the bottom of the furnace. The Karita Power Station in Japan uses this technology.

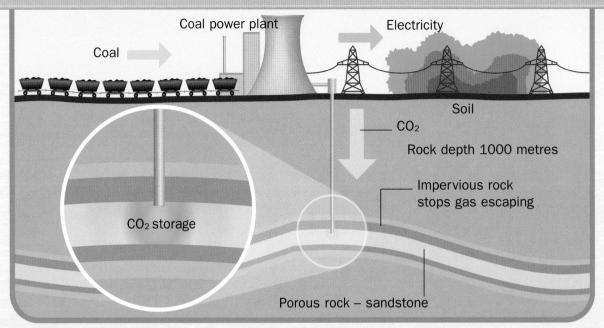

Coal power plant

Coal

Electricity

Soil

CO_2

Rock depth 1000 metres

Impervious rock
stops gas escaping

CO_2 storage

Porous rock – sandstone

Carbon capture

Carbon capture Carbon emissions can be reduced by capturing and storing the carbon dioxide produced by burning fossil fuels. This is known as carbon capture and storage. Carbon dioxide capture has been achieved on a small scale, but improvements need to be made before it can work in power stations. Once captured, the carbon would be stored underground in old mines, aquifers or in the rocks from which oil has been extracted.

Different storing techniques

Technologies under development include post-combustion capture (removing carbon dioxide from exhaust gases in the power station chimney), pre-combustion capture and oxyfuel combustion (where coal is burned in pure oxygen instead of air, producing almost pure carbon dioxide). Currently,

One idea for carbon capture is to pump the carbon dioxide from burning coal into porous rock layers deep underground. Impervious layers of rocks above stop the gas escaping.

post-combustion capture uses special solvents that absorb carbon dioxide. The most common solvents are chemicals called amines. Other technologies are being investigated, including membranes with microscopic holes that allow other gases through, but trap the carbon dioxide. The captured carbon dioxide would be pumped down into the ground for storage, or combined with special materials to form new minerals, so trapping the carbon dioxide forever.

Experimental 'zero-emissions' power plants are on the horizon. For example, the Canadian Clean Power Coalition is planning a coal-fired power station with carbon capture for 2010.

Turning coal into gas In future, we may not burn coal, but instead convert it into gases. Engineers are testing a system called the integrated gasification combined cycle (IGCC), which burns gas from coal or oil to generate electricity. There are several experimental power plants of this kind already being built around the world, including FutureGen in the USA and Sarlux in Italy. These plants are much more efficient and cleaner than coal-burning power stations. In time, this technology could be used in zero-emission power stations. The system would produce hydrogen for burning and carbon dioxide, which would be captured and stored.

Japanese scientists are developing a similar technology, called the integrated gasification fuel cell (IGFC). Here, the hydrogen powers fuel cells that generate electricity (see chapter 5 for more about fuel cells). A commercial IGFC station should be running in Japan by 2020.

HOW IT WORKS

In an IGCC power station, coal is heated to a high temperature, but not burned. It combines with steam and oxygen to form a gas called syngas, which is mainly hydrogen. The syngas is burned in a gas turbine, which operates an electricity generator.

Part of the Sarlux IGCC power plant on the island of Sardinia, Italy. It converts waste oil from a nearby refinery into gases, which are burned to generate electricity.

CHAPTER 3
new fuels

As fossil fuel supplies start to dwindle, new fuels will take their place. Two of the most important are fuels from plants (biomass and biofuels) and hydrogen. Wood has been a fuel source for thousands of years, but today special energy crops are being grown.

At the Agricultural Research Centre, Maryland, USA, the visitor bus is fuelled by soy diesel made from the soya bean biocrops growing in the fields.

Electricity from biomass Two technologies allow biomass to be burned in electricity generating stations. In direct-firing, biomass is burned in the station's furnace. In co-firing, biomass is mixed with coal before burning. Co-firing is already

BIO-TERMS

The terms biomass, biofuel and bioenergy mean different things.

- Biomass is any organic material used to produce energy. It includes purpose-grown plants, known as energy (or bioenergy) crops, waste from the forestry and paper industries, green waste and manure. A biomass fuel is biomass burned as fuel.
- A biofuel is a liquid fuel or gas fuel produced from biomass using chemical or biological processes.
- Bioenergy is the energy released when biomass fuels or biofuels are burned.

HOW IT WORKS

Biological, chemical and thermal processes are used to make biofuels. For example, ethanol is made from corn. The corn is ground up, cooked and then fermented. During fermentation, yeast breaks the chemicals in the corn into ethanol and other chemicals. Methane is made from manure and other wastes in a process called anaerobic digestion. The wastes are broken down by bacteria and other microorganisms.

in use in dozens of power stations. It is a good way of using current coal-fired stations to burn biomass, and is an efficient way of getting the energy from the biomass. Small-scale systems for producing electricity from biomass will become useful for villages, farms and

small factories in remote areas, where there is plenty of biomass but no grid electricity supply.

Biofuels Biofuels are made from biomass. The main biofuels are methanol, ethanol, biodiesel and methane, which are burned in vehicle engines, electricity generators and in industrial processes. Crops such as bamboo and willow are used to make biofuel. They are genetically modified to make them grow more quickly, and so that they contain chemicals that can easily be converted to fuel. Biofuels are already widely available in Europe, the USA and Brazil. The European Union has set a target of five per cent biofuel use in transport by 2010. This technology will continue to be used as bioenergy crops become more widespread.

A small plant in Linkoping, Sweden that produces biogas (made up mainly of methane) from animal waste.

FOR AND AGAINST

For

- Biofuels come from plants, which take in carbon dioxide as they grow, so they are 'carbon neutral'.
- Biofuels are renewable fuels when more plants are grown to replace them.
- Biodiesel burns more cleanly than diesel made from crude oil.
- Some biomass fuels and biofuels are made from waste.

Against

- Growing and processing biofuel crops on a large scale could lead to increased food prices because less land is used for growing food crops.
- Some biofuels, such as ethanol, create more pollution than fossil fuels when they are burned.

Rubbish into fuel We may soon even be turning rubbish into fuel. Processes called pyrolysis and gasification allow agricultural, forestry and household waste to be turned into fuels. In pyrolysis, waste is heated in an airtight container, which makes it release oil and gas without burning. The oil and gas can be burned to generate electricity. At present, pyrolysis is inefficient because energy is needed to heat the waste. In gasification, waste is heated with a little air, which makes the waste release a gas called syngas. This can power a gas turbine or furnace to generate electricity. Gasification could become more efficient than direct-firing (see page 16). Both pyrolysis and gasification are in use on a small scale in hundreds of plants

Harvesting willow which has been grown as an energy crop. The willow will be taken to a processing plant to be turned into fuels, or burned in power stations.

A robot filling arm refuels a car with hydrogen gas at Munich airport, Germany.

around the world, and large-scale plants are being tested in Europe and Japan.

Hydrogen as a fuel Hydrogen is often talked about as the fuel of the future. When it burns, it produces only water and no carbon dioxide. It can be used in fuel cells to produce electricity. However, there is no natural supply of hydrogen on Earth, so we have to make it. Currently, hydrogen is produced from natural gas, or by splitting up water using electricity. However, both these methods use lots of energy. Currently, there are a few hydrogen filling stations for hydrogen-powered cars, dotted about in North America, Europe and Japan, but before hydrogen can replace other fuels, we will need infrastructure to produce and distribute it on a large scale.

WHAT'S NEXT?

Several new hydrogen-producing technologies are in development. These technologies will allow us to make hydrogen using renewable energy sources. One example is the photogeneration cell, which uses solar energy to convert water to hydrogen and oxygen. Another is the bioreactor, which uses genetically modified algae to produce hydrogen. Complex mixtures of natural chemicals called enzymes could also produce hydrogen from starch (a chemical found in biomass such as woodchips).

CHAPTER 4
water, wind and rocks

Water flowing down rivers, ocean currents, waves and wind all have kinetic energy that we can capture and convert to electricity. These are all renewable, emission-free sources of energy. Rocks deep underground also contain heat energy that we can bring to the surface.

We already harness all these forms of energy, but they will be more important as oil runs out. New technologies will allow us to capture this energy more efficiently and in greater quantities.

Hydroelectricity Hydroelectricity is electricity generated from the energy in flowing water. At the moment it provides more energy than all the other renewable energies combined. Hydroelectric technology is very efficient, and is unlikely to change much in the future, except that small-scale and micro-scale hydroelectric plants, that provide energy for small communities and farms, are likely to become more common.

Energy from tides Tidal energy is the energy in water currents caused by the rise and fall of the tide. Current tidal power stations use barrages (like dams) placed across estuaries to trap rising and falling water, and allow it to flow through turbines. A new idea being developed is the tidal lagoon,

which is like a circular barrage. Water flows into the lagoon as the tide rises and drains out through turbines as it falls. Tidal lagoons are proposed for Swansea Bay in the UK and the Yellow Sea in northeast China.

Most future tidal energy is likely to be based on tidal turbines (also called

FOR AND AGAINST

For
- Tidal energy is a clean and renewable energy source.
- Tidal energy is reliable: you can predict how much energy will be produced at specific times of the day.

Against
- Current tidal barrages interrupt the natural flow of water, which can harm marine animals and plants.
- Underwater turbines and fences could be a hazard for shipping and large marine animals.

tidal mills). These sit in the water and capture the energy in currents with rotors. There are some prototypes working, and new devices being developed. For example, there are six turbines in New York's East River, and Marine Current Turbines has installed the world's largest tidal turbine in Northern Ireland. Both are producing electricity for homes as they are tested.

The illustration below shows what a field of free-flow turbines looks like under water. This is the kind of turbine used in the East River, New York, USA.

WHAT'S NEXT?

For large-scale electricity generation, dozens or even hundreds of tidal turbines will work together. They will either be spread throughout a channel of water, or placed side by side to create a structure called a tidal fence. A large tidal fence, with hundreds of turbines, could generate several gigawatts of electricity. Just one gigawatt is enough to power 500,000 homes. If Northern Ireland's prototype turbine is successful, a tidal farm is planned for around 2011.

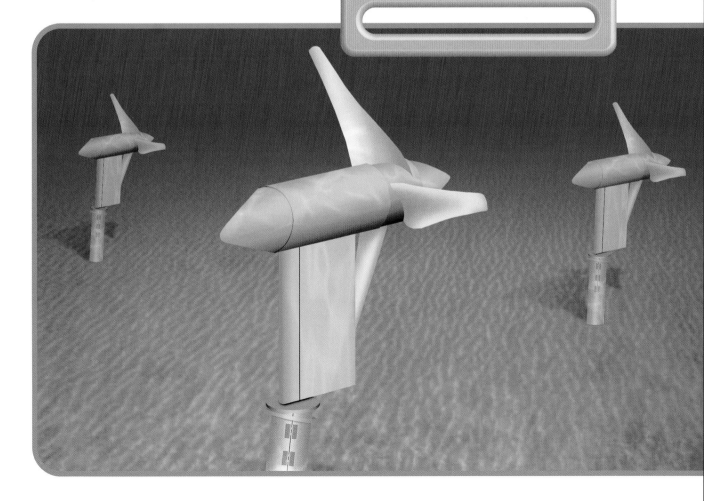

Energy from ocean waves Waves have energy in them because water moves up and down as a wave passes by. Engineers have designed many different devices for capturing wave energy, but so far, none have been used to generate electricity on a large scale. Three systems currently under test are the Pelamis, Wave Dragon and PowerBuoy. These systems may be producing electricity commercially in the next ten years.

A Pelamis wave-energy machine during trials in the North Sea. Passing waves cause the joints to bend, which pumps fluid to a turbine.

Waves move across the sea and cause the Pelamis to rise and fall in a snake-like motion.

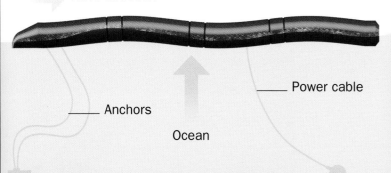

Wave direction

Anchors

Ocean

Power cable

HOW IT WORKS

The Pelamis system, designed by Ocean Power Delivery in the UK, consists of four long floats connected end-to-end by flexible joints. Each joint contains a hydraulic pump. As waves move the joints, oil is pumped from the joints through motors, which in turn drive generators that produce electricity. A square kilometre of ocean can provide 30 megawatts of power – enough to run 20,000 homes.

A PowerBuoy, made by Ocean Power Technologies, under test. The PowerBuoy pumps fluid to a turbine as it bobs up and down in the waves.

Heat from the ocean The top layers of the oceans are warmed by the Sun, while lower layers stay very cold. This difference in temperature can be used to generate electricity using a technology called ocean thermal energy conversion (OTEC). This is a renewable energy source because it captures energy from the Sun. Experimental OTEC plants have been built in Japan and Hawaii but the technology is too expensive at the moment to produce electricity commercially.

HOW IT WORKS

There is a difference of between 10 and 20°C between the temperature at the ocean surface and a kilometre down below it. In one design of OTEC, called a closed-cycle system, warm surface water is used to heat a special fluid, making the fluid boil. The gas formed drives a turbine and generator. Then cold water from deep in the ocean cools the gas, turning it back to liquid to be used again.

Geothermal energy The heat in rocks can be used for heating water and generating electricity. Current technologies work only in volcanic areas of the world, where there is hot rock near the surface. Hot-dry-rock (HDR) technology is a way of gathering geothermal energy anywhere in the world. An HDR system needs pipes that reach several kilometres into the ground, where rocks are naturally warm. Water is fed down the pipes to be heated, so gathering the heat energy. Experimental systems are being developed in France, Japan and Australia, but commercial systems are many years away. In theory, this technology could provide all our energy needs for thousands of years to come.

Wind energy Wind turbines and wind farms (made up of tens or hundreds of turbines) capture the energy in wind and turn it into electricity. Wind turbines are already a successful technology, but engineers are trying to develop more efficient turbines, and turbines that will work at low wind speeds. They hope that the wind could produce about 30 per cent of the world's electricity by 2030.

The larger a turbine rotor is, the more energy the turbine can gather. The latest generation of large turbines have rotors made with advanced composite materials, so that they can be long and rigid without being too heavy. For example, the RE Power 5M has glass- and carbon-fibre blades. At the Sandia National

A simplified diagram of the inside of a wind turbine nacelle, the bullet-shaped container where all a wind turbine's machinery is located. Other parts in a wind turbine turn the nacelle to face the wind.

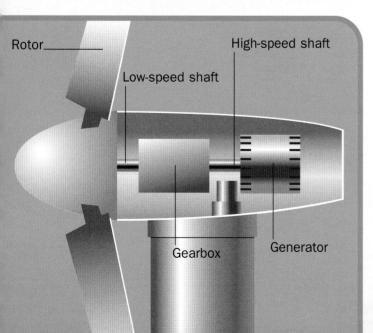

Turbines at the Trimont Wind Farm, Minnesota, USA. Each of the 67 turbines here produces 1.5 megawatts of power. Farming continues under the turbines.

Laboratories in the USA, researchers are investigating adaptive rotors. These rotors have blades that change shape under computer control as the wind speed changes, allowing them to make the most efficient use of low, medium and high wind speeds.

FOR AND AGAINST

For
- Wind energy is a clean, renewable, source of energy.
- Wind farms take up only a little space on the ground.
- Wind farms can be built out at sea, where the wind is more reliable.
- The energy used to build a wind farm is produced by that farm within four to six months. After that, the energy it produces is free.

Against
- Wind turbines stop when the wind stops.
- Currently, electricity from wind farms is more expensive than energy from fossil-fuel power stations.

WHAT'S NEXT?

Thousands of metres above the ground, winds are normally stronger and less gusty, which is better for wind turbines. Engineers have designed experimental airborne turbines, which fly high above the ground to capture these winds. For example, the Magenn Power Air Rotor is a helium-filled turbine that floats in the air, designed in Canada. At the moment, lack of funding for these projects means there is no commercial system.

A giant RE Power 5M turbine – the world's largest – being assembled in the North Sea.

Mega turbines Wind turbines continue to grow in size, with larger rotors supported on taller towers. At present, the world's largest turbine is the RE Power 5M machine. Its rotor has three 61.5 metre composite blades. In a good breeze, it produces five megawatts of power — enough to supply about 4,000 houses. Such 5M machines are being tested in the North Sea, and are due to be used for an offshore wind farm in the Baltic in 2008.

CHAPTER 5
cells and batteries

Cells and batteries contain stores of energy in chemical form. A battery is made up of two or more cells joined together. Cells and batteries are used as portable sources of energy in devices such as mobile phones, watches and laptop computers.

Batteries are also used to store energy (such as the energy from wind turbines), and to start engines and drive electric vehicles. Battery researchers are always trying to improve what they call power density. This means developing smaller, lighter batteries that store as much energy as possible. This is particularly important for devices such as mobile phones and laptop computers, which need increasing amounts of energy to

Good battery life (how long a battery supplies power for before running down) is critical for portable devices such as laptop computers.

FOR AND AGAINST

For
- Batteries are portable stores of energy.
- Batteries provide a useful energy back-up in case other sources fail.

Against
- Current batteries store only a limited amount of electricity.
- Most batteries contain toxic chemicals, such as cadmium, that must be disposed of carefully.
- Some batteries can overheat and catch fire.
- Some new battery technologies could mean electronic devices have to be redesigned before the batteries can power them.

power their advanced features. It is also important for electric and hybrid cars, which need lightweight and powerful batteries to drive them. Devices called fuel cells may replace batteries in many machines in the future.

Current battery technology

Batteries are classed as primary (which cannot be recharged) or secondary (which are rechargeable). Different types of battery use different chemicals to store and release energy. The most common disposable batteries are zinc-carbon and alkaline, and the most common rechargeable batteries are nickel metal hydride, nickel cadmium and lithium ion.

Of these, lithium ion batteries have the best power density, and are used in all mobile phones and laptop computers. Lithium polymer (Li-Poly) batteries can be made in very thin, flexible sheets, and in almost any shape. Now Li-Poly batteries that can be recharged in minutes are being developed. Thin-film batteries use Li-Poly technology. They are made by printing the battery materials onto a base material, such as silicon, plastic or paper. Thin-film batteries are currently only used in specialist applications,

High-power-density Li-Poly batteries are useful for model aircraft, where weight must be kept to a minimum.

HOW IT WORKS

All batteries have two parts called electrodes, each made of a different material. Between the electrodes is a material called an electrolyte. The materials work together to produce electricity when the battery is connected to an electric circuit. In a lithium polymer battery, the electrodes are made from two different materials that contain the chemical lithium. The electrolyte is contained in a special plastic (which is the polymer). When the battery is connected, lithium ions move through the electrolyte, carrying electricity.

such as medical implants. Another new battery type is the zinc matrix battery, which can store twice the energy of a lithium ion battery.

Flow batteries The flow battery is a type of battery that will become important for storing the large amounts of energy from renewable sources of energy, such as solar cells and wind turbines. In a flow battery, used chemicals are pumped out of the battery container as electricity is drawn from it, and are replaced by fresh chemicals. The battery provides electricity as long as new chemicals are pumped in. During recharging, the chemicals are pumped in the reverse direction, which refreshes them.

Another battery technology under development is the molten-salt battery, which has both a very high energy density and a high power output. It may prove to be useful for grid energy storage and in electric vehicles, but the salt material must be heated at 400-700°C for the battery to work. More research is needed to make molten-salt batteries safe to use. At present, these batteries are used only by the military.

Wireless recharging One of the drawbacks of battery-powered devices is that the batteries must be recharged

WHAT'S NEXT?

The amazing developments happening in nanotechnology promise to improve how batteries work. The larger a battery's electrodes, the more electricity it can store, the faster it can give out its electricity, and the faster it can be recharged. An electrode covered with microscopic nanotowers has a much larger surface area than a flat electrode. When fully developed, this technology will allow many times more electricity to be stored in small, light batteries.

An electron microscope photograph shows a carbon nanotower.

regularly by plugging the device into mains electricity. A new technology is wireless charging. The technology is similar to that used in electric toothbrush chargers where the toothbrush slots into the charger, but no electrical contact is made. However, wireless charging will work simply by placing the device on a pad. Two companies, Splashpower in the UK, and WildCharge in the USA have developed wireless charging pads. In a few years, wireless charging could work even when a device is several metres from a charging unit, which would be in a wall or on the floor. Once in range, charging would start automatically.

Fuel cells A fuel cell produces electricity from a reaction between a fuel and a chemical called an oxidant. For example, in a hydrogen fuel cell,

A charging mat called the SplashPad from manufacturer SplashPower. Devices placed on the pad recharge automatically.

The solar-electric Helios Prototype, built by NASA, is powered by solar cells by day and a fuel cell at night.

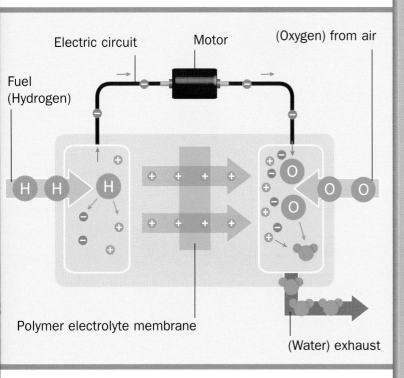

Electric circuit · Motor · (Oxygen) from air

Fuel (Hydrogen)

Polymer electrolyte membrane

(Water) exhaust

In a fuel cell, hydrogen (on the left) reacts with oxygen (on the right) inside the electrolyte. The hydrogen splits into + ions and – electrons. The – electrons flow through the circuit as electric current and power the motor.

HOW IT WORKS

A fuel cell changes chemical energy into electrical energy. A common type of fuel cell uses hydrogen gas as a fuel, and oxygen gas as an oxidiser (an oxidiser removes electrons, or charged particles, during a chemical reaction). The hydrogen and oxygen react in a solution of potassium hydroxide in water (this is called the electrolyte). During the reaction, electrons move between electrodes (electric terminals) inside the fuel cell, causing an electric current to flow. The current continues so long as hydrogen and oxygen continue to be added to the cell. A by-product of the process is water.

the fuel is hydrogen and the oxidant is oxygen. The reaction converts the energy in the fuel into electricity. As the fuel and oxidant in the cell is used up, more is added, so the cell keeps working as long as fuel and oxidant are supplied to it. Fuel cells are already in use in place of batteries in specialist applications, such as satellites, remote weather stations, military devices and some electric cars, but further research

and development is needed to make them cheap and easy to use.

Existing fuel-cell technology

The most common fuel in use is the polymer electrolyte membrane fuel cell (PEMFC). This fuel cell normally uses hydrogen and oxygen, but other fuels and oxidants are also used, such as methanol and oxygen. Currently, fuel cells are expensive to make because the materials used for the electrodes and membranes are costly. They are used only where their

A direct methanol fuel cell made by the Toshiba Corporation to power portable electronic devices. It weighs just 8.5 grams.

expense can be justified, such as portable military devices and vehicles, in spacecraft and for power back-up in hospitals. However, as research continues, they are becoming cheaper. Compact methanol fuel cells for portable devices are being developed, which work with simple fuel canisters. Demonstration cells have powered devices for ten times longer than batteries the same size.

WHAT'S NEXT?

Many new types of fuel cell, each using different combinations of chemicals, are being developed. Near-future developments include fuel cells made from biodegradable materials, which will be cheap and disposable, and sugar-fuelled cells. The widespread use of fuel cells will depend on the availability of hydrogen as a fuel (see chapter 3).

CHAPTER 6
solar energy

Solar energy is heat and light energy that comes from the Sun. Solar energy technology allows us to catch this energy and use it for heating and generating electricity.

Solar energy will keep coming to the Earth for billions of years, so solar energy is renewable. In fact, because the Sun's heat drives the weather, wind energy, hydroelectric energy and wave energy ultimately come from the Sun.

LIMITLESS ENERGY

The Sun gives out a staggering amount of energy in the form of heat, light and other forms of radiation (such as ultra-violet radiation). It is estimated that it produces 400 million billion billion joules every second. Only about half a billionth of this energy hits the Earth, but even so, if we could capture it all for just a minute, we would have enough energy for all our needs for more than a year.

A solar-powered parking-ticket machine in a street in Nottingham, England. The machine uses no other power source.

Solar cells A solar cell (also called a photovoltaic cell, or PV cell) converts light from the Sun directly into electricity. Individual solar cells don't produce much power, and are normally combined together to form solar arrays or solar panels. Solar cells already have many different applications, from powering watches and calculators to generating electricity at solar power stations.

WHAT'S NEXT?

An idea that sounds like science fiction, but that is being researched by NASA, is the solar satellite. The satellite would orbit high above the Earth, where it would be in sunshine 24 hours a day. It would have a solar panel a kilometre or more across, and send the energy collected down to Earth by microwaves, which would be collected by an antenna about 10 kilometres across. The main problem facing NASA is the huge cost of launching the parts of the satellite into space.

Solar cells in buildings Solar panels can be added to the roof of any building to provide electricity. However, many modern, environmentally friendly buildings are being designed with solar panels built in. These are known as building-integrated photovoltaics (BIPV). The building materials, such as

This giant disk floating in space is what a solar satellite may look like. It could harvest energy from the Sun for a variety of possible uses back on Earth.

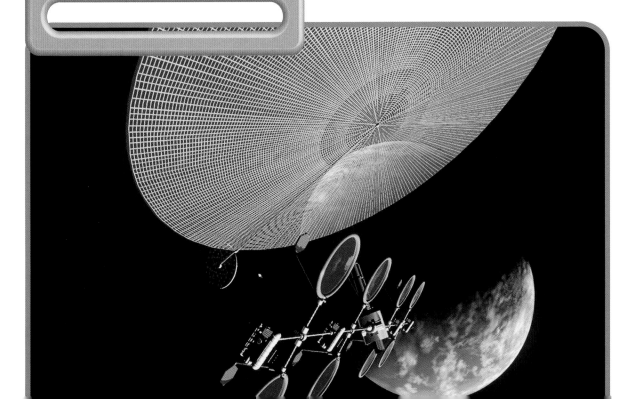

An 'energy roof' at a supermarket in England. Solar cells form part of the roof. This is an example of building-integrated photovoltaics (BIPVs).

FOR AND AGAINST

For
- After solar cells and panels are paid for, solar energy is free.
- Solar cells and panels do not create pollution or carbon emissions.
- Solar technology is useful in remote areas.
- Solar cells are very reliable.

Against
- Current solar cells are expensive.
- No energy is produced at night, or in places that get little sunshine.
- Solar panels can look ugly, especially on the roofs of old buildings.

roof tiles, wall cladding and glass can include solar panels. The solar panels can be grid connected, which means that any electricity they produce that is not used in the building itself is fed into the electricity grid.

Solar-cell power stations The first power stations that use solar cells to generate electricity are working. These solar 'farms' have hundreds or thousands of solar panels that follow the Sun as it moves across the sky. An experimental solar power station in Victoria, Australia, will eventually provide electricity for 45,000 homes. A station planned in Ontario, Canada, using more than a million solar panels, should produce 40 megawatts of power by 2010.

Solar-cell technology Current solar cells (known as first-generation cells) are made from silicon semiconductors. Even the best ones convert just 20 per cent of the light energy that hits them into electricity. They only collect energy from a part of the light spectrum. They are also expensive to make, and a solar panel takes many years to pay for itself with the money saved on buying batteries or mains electricity. However, researchers are developing new types of cell that are cheaper and more efficient.

Second-generation solar cells are in production. They also use silicon semiconductors, but these can be coated onto flexible materials, rather than being in solid cells. They are cheaper than first-generation cells, but so far only half as efficient. Third-generation solar cells are also being developed. They use new types of semiconductor materials. One type is based on plastics, and is known as an organic solar cell. These are cheaper and lighter than silicon-based cells, and are easy to integrate into other materials, such as glass. Fourth-generation cells promise to be far more efficient than other cells. They will be made up of many layers that collect energy from the whole spectrum of light.

Nanotechnology is also being applied to solar cells. Experimental solar cells, known as 3D solar cells, are covered with millions of microscopic towers about 0.1 mm across. These can capture light more efficiently than flat cells.

A senior research engineer at the Georgia Tech Research Institute, USA, holds a solar cell built with nanotechnology, known as a 3D solar cell.

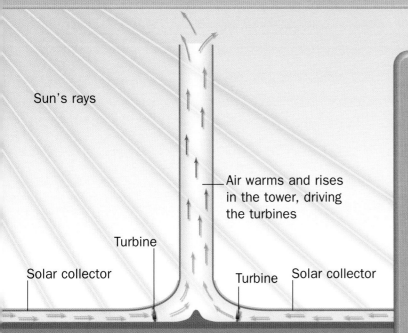

Sun's rays

Air warms and rises in the tower, driving the turbines

Turbine

Solar collector

Turbine

Solar collector

The inside of a proposed solar tower. The tower would be twice as high as the world's tallest existing structure, the CN Tower.

WHAT'S NEXT?

Research is progressing into the idea of collecting solar thermal energy with structures called solar towers. A solar tower would work on the principle that hot air rises. A proposed solar tower would have a central tower up to a kilometre high, with a greenhouse-like collector several kilometres across at the base. Heat from the Sun would heat air in the collector, which would rise up the tower, making turbines at the base of the tower spin.

WHAT'S NEXT?

Several solar-cell technologies may appear in the near future, which will help to make solar energy more commonplace. For example, special dual-purpose screens for mobile phones and laptops could contain solar cells that would generate the electricity needed to run the display. Solar breeder technology is an idea in which energy from solar cells, rather than from burning fossil fuels, is used in the production of more solar cells. Solar energy may also help to produce fuels such as hydrogen and biodiesel (see chapter 3).

Solar thermal energy Solar thermal technology works in a different way to solar cells. It captures heat energy from the Sun (the same heat that you feel on your face on a sunny day). Currently, the main use of solar thermal energy is for heating hot water in homes. Flat panel collectors trap the Sun's heat and use it to heat the water, which is stored in a hot water tank. Advanced systems have water pipes in a vacuum, which stops the heat escaping by convection. Passive solar heating (see chapter 1) is another way of capturing solar thermal energy.

Solar thermal energy is also used to generate electricity. There is a state-of-the-art solar thermal power station in

Andalusia, Spain. This is Europe's first commercial solar thermal power station. It has 600 mirrors that concentrate heat onto a tower, producing 11 MW of power (enough for about 6,000 homes). The station will eventually be enlarged to provide electricity for the whole of Seville.

An aerial view of the Solucar solar power station in Spain. The 600 mirrors in the background focus heat onto the tower. In the foreground are solar cells that produce electricity, similar to those found on buildings.

HOW IT WORKS

At a solar thermal power station, the Sun's rays are collected by mirrors that focus them onto the top of a tower. The mirrors (which are also called heliostats) track the Sun as it moves across the sky, and work together like a giant curved mirror. This heats water in boilers in the tower, creating steam. The steam turns turbines, which turn electricity generators.

CHAPTER 7
nuclear energy

Nuclear energy is energy captured from nuclear reactions. There are two types of nuclear reaction: fission and fusion.

At the moment, all nuclear power stations produce electricity from nuclear fission. Nuclear fusion is proving to be quite a challenge. It is being researched, but commercial fusion power stations are decades away still. In the meantime, some countries are building new fission power stations because their politicians believe nuclear energy is the most reliable alternative to fossil fuels.

Nuclear fission In nuclear fission, energy is released when an atom splits apart to make two smaller atoms. In a nuclear power station, the reactions take place inside the reactor. Here, uranium atoms split up, giving off heat

HOW MUCH ENERGY?

During a nuclear reaction, some matter in the atoms is turned to energy. A tiny amount of matter turns into an incredible amount of energy. For example, one gram of matter changes into nearly 100 million million joules, enough to run a light bulb for 32,000 years!

The Brokdorf nuclear power station, near the city of Hamburg in Germany, produces 1.4 gigawatts. The reactor inside is a pressurized water reactor (PWR).

FOR AND AGAINST

For
- Nuclear fission creates large amounts of energy.
- The reactors do not release carbon emissions in the atmosphere.

Against
- Nuclear fission produces highly dangerous, long-lasting radioactive waste, which must be buried deep underground for thousands of years.
- A major accident, or terrorist attack at a nuclear power station could release deadly radiation.
- Uranium fuel has to be mined from underground.
- There is a limited supply of uranium for current reactors of between 50 and 100 years.
- Reactors are extremely expensive to build and to dismantle at the end of their lives, and some parts become radioactive waste.

A European water reactor (EWR or ERP) currently under construction at Olkiluoto in Finland.

energy. This produces steam to drive turbines, which turn electricity generators. There are several different types of reactor, but the most common is the pressurized water reactor (PWR). New reactor designs, such as the advanced pressurized water reactor and European water reactor (EWR), are based on this design. These are known as generation III reactors. Near-future reactors are generation III+ reactors. Several are in the process of being designed and tested by commercial companies, such as General Electric in the USA, Westinghouse in Germany, and Mitsubishi in Japan. They are generally simpler to build and run, cheaper, safer and more efficient than current reactors.

Nuclear fusion Nuclear fusion is the fusion (joining together) of two atomic nuclei to form a new, larger nucleus. It's the nuclear reaction that happens in the Sun. Fusion does not just happen. Two nuclei must be smashed into each other at incredible speed to make them fuse. This requires temperatures of millions of degrees centigrade and immense pressures, which are very hard to create. However, if scientists can make fusion work, we will have a source of limitless, clean energy.

Fusion research There are two main technical problems to overcome. The first is to generate the temperature required for fusion, which is ten times the temperature in the centre of the Sun because the pressure there is far greater than what can be recreated on Earth. The second is to make a container that can both stop the fast-moving nuclei and other particles from escaping, and stand up to the immense heat.

HOW IT WORKS

In a proposed fusion reactor, the fuel would be heated to millions of degrees by lasers. The atoms on the fuel would then form a material called a plasma, containing fast-moving nuclei. When two nuclei collide, they would fuse together, releasing heat. The heat would be absorbed by a liquid around the reactor, and the liquid would heat water to produce steam for turbines.

The Joint European Torus (JET) is the largest fusion research reactor built so far. Inside, the nuclei of hydrogen atoms are fused to form helium nuclei. The particles are contained in a device

Inside the Joint European Torus (JET). This is the chamber where the fusion reactions take place.

FOR AND AGAINST

For

- Nuclear fusion could provide limitless energy for thousands of years.
- Fusion is much safer than fission, as it cannot run out of control.
- Fusion does not produce dangerous radioactive wastes.

Against

- Working fusion reactors are decades away.
- Research and development will be vastly expensive.
- Fusion reactors will become radioactive.

WHAT'S NEXT?

Construction of the International Thermonuclear Experimental Reactor (ITER) is due to begin in France in 2008. Its design is similar to, but more advanced than the JET. It will take 10 years to build, and 20 years of research will follow. Success is not guaranteed, as the reactor may be too expensive to run. However, if ITER does work, there are plans to build a demonstration power plant, which would start producing electricity around 2035.

called a tokamak. This produces a doughnut-shaped magnetic field that stops the particles escaping. The JET has produced fusion for a split second, but more energy is needed to operate it than it releases. Two other research projects, in the USA and in the UK, use lasers to compress and heat hydrogen to very high temperatures.

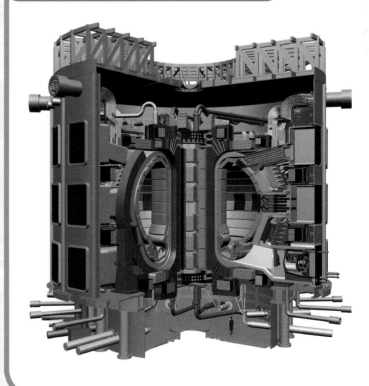

A computer model of the future experimental International Thermonuclear Experimental Reactor (ITER). The fusing particles would be in the central doughnut-shaped space.

conclusion

This book has discussed a wide range of energy technologies, some that are in use now, some that will come into use in the near future, and some that we will have to wait decades to see.

Perhaps some of the technologies covered, such as solar satellites and nuclear fusion, may never work. We need new energy technologies for several reasons. Some technologies, such as advanced batteries and wireless charging, will make our everyday lives more convenient. We will be forced to use other technologies, such as clean coal and wave power, as our reserves of oil run out. But the main reason is to reduce carbon emissions. Developing these low-carbon technologies is a job for scientists and engineers, but if we are going to use them on a large scale, governments must help to pay for the research, and encourage people to use them.

What's obvious is that we must begin to use more low-carbon technologies to produce our energy, and we must do it straight away. It is the only way that we will avert the disasters that runaway global warming could bring.

Long-term visions So how will we be getting all the energy we need in 30 years' time? It is almost impossible to

CARBON FREE?

Some experts argue that renewable energy sources are not emission free, as they are sometimes thought to be. This is because of the energy needed to build and operate them. Renewable energy is not initially free, because it costs money to build wind turbines, hydroelectric dams and so on. However a windfarm pays for itself in as little as four months and a photovoltaic panel pays for itself in three years. From then on, the energy they produce is carbon free.

predict accurately, but if the technologies we have investigated here reach their potential, then things will be very different to today:

• Most of our electricity will come from renewable sources, such as giant offshore wind farms and wave farms, solar-cell and solar thermal power stations, and perhaps even solar towers and satellites.

- Fuel cells will provide the electricity for our cars and mobile devices, and you will fill up with hydrogen or methanol at the filling station.

- Many of us will live in zero-carbon homes that will not release carbon into the atmosphere.

- Coal-fired power stations may still be operating, but will be emission free.

- Our energy supply may be rationed, where credit card-type technologies keep track of how much energy we use.

- We may even be using electricity from the first nuclear fusion power stations.

In the future, new homes could look like the Millennium Eco-House at the University of Nottingham, England. Energy-efficient technologies include solar cells, solar panels, a wind turbine, combined heat and power (CHP) and natural lighting.

Some of these ideas may seem like science fiction to us today, but 30 years ago, much of the technology we have today was science fiction. In the next century, our energy may come from technologies that nobody has even thought about. The challenge is to change the way we use energy as well as developing new sources of energy.

glossary

anaerobic Describes a process that happens without oxygen (for example an anaerobic digester produces methane from animal dung without air, in an airtight container).

aquifer A layer of rock underground that contains water. The rock in aquifers is porous and permeable, meaning that it is full of tiny holes that water can flow into and out of.

biodiesel A renewable fuel made from plant-based oils, often combined with diesel made from crude oil.

carbon emissions Any carbon dioxide and methane that is released into the air by the combustion of fuels.

combustion The burning process inside an engine.

electron One of the tiny particles that make up an atom. Electrons orbit around the central nucleus of an atom. They also are the particles that make up an electric current in a wire.

emission What is produced when an engine burns.

fossil fuel A fuel formed from the remains of ancient animals and plants that have been altered by heat and pressure underground. Coal, oil and gas are the main fossil fuels.

fuel cell Chemical device for making electricity.

generator A device that produces electricity when its central armature is turned. It turns movement energy into electricity.

genetic modification The manipulation of the genes in a plant or animal to improve the characteristics of that plant or animal's genes. (Genes are the chemical codes in an organism that control the structure and function of cells.)

global warming The gradual warming of the Earth's atmosphere, caused by carbon emissions.

impervious A substance that does not absorb water.

kinetic energy Movement energy.

microchip A computer processor contained on an integrated-circuit chip.

molecule The smallest particle of a substance that can exist and still keep the properties of the substance. Most molecules are made up of two or more atoms joined together. For example, a water molecule contains one oxygen and two hydrogen atoms.

nanotechnology The design and manufacture of extremely small devices by building them with individual atoms and molecules.

nuclear fission A nuclear reaction in which the nucleus (central part) of an atom splits apart.

nuclear fusion A nuclear reaction in which the nuclei of two atoms fuse together.

oxidant A chemical that supplies oxygen in a chemical reaction. For example, oxygen is the oxidant when a fuel burns.

polymer A material made up from molecules that are long chains of atoms. The chains are made up from many small molecules (called monomers) joined together.

proton One of the two tiny particles that make up the nucleus (central part) of an atom (the other is called the neutron).

semiconductor A material that allows electricity to pass through it gradually.

superconducting Describes a material that has no electrical resistance, so that electricity flows through it extremely easily.

syngas A gas made by heating coal, biomass or organic waste without letting it burn. It is made up mostly of hydrogen and carbon dioxide.

turbine 1. A device containing fans that spin when steam or burning gas pass through it, used in power stations to drive an electricity generator, or **2.** a device with a rotor that turns because of wind or flowing water.

further information

Books

Action for the Environment: Energy Supplies by Chris Oxlade, Franklin Watts, 2004.

Dilemmas in Modern Science: Power by Kate Ravilious, Evans, 2008.

Sustainable Futures: Energy by John Stringer, Evans, 2006.

Science Essentials Chemistry: Fuels and the Environment by Denise Walker, Evans, 2007.

Science in Focus: The Earth's Resources by Richard and Louise Spilsbury, Evans, 2006.

Websites

Website of the Centre for Renewable Energy and Sustainable Technology.
www.crest.org

This website looks at the different energy sources of the oceans.
www.oceanrenewable.com

Places to visit

The Science Museum
Exhibition Road, South Kensington, London SW7 2DD www.sciencemuseum.org.uk/

Glasgow Science Centre
50 Pacific Quay, Glasgow, G51 1EA www.glasgowsciencecentre.org/

Centre for Alternative Technology
Machynlleth, Powys SY20 9AZ www.cat.org.uk

Eureka!
Discovery Rd, Halifax HX1 2NE www.eureka.org.uk

Manchester Museum of Science and Industry
Liverpool Road, Castlefield, Manchester www.msim.org.uk

Cruachan Visitor Centre
(hydroelectric power station)
Dalmally, Argyll PA33 1AN

Sellafield Visitors Centre
(nuclear power station)
Sellafield, Seascale, Cumbria CA20 www.visitcumbria.com/wc/svc.htm

Scroby Sands wind farm information centre
North Drive, Great Yarmouth, Norfolk NR30 1ED

Electric mountain (hydroelectric power station)
Llanberis, Gwynedd, LL55 4TY www.electricmountain.co.uk/electric_mountain.htm

index